HEALTHY DIET

by Rebecca Phillips-Bartlett

Minneapolis, Minnesota

Credits

Images are courtesy of Shutterstock.com. With thanks to Getty Images, ThinkstockPhoto, and iStockphoto. Recurring images – gravity_point, inspiring. team, Gaidamashchuk, Zakharchenko Anna. Cover – Brovko Serhii, Elena Elisseeva. 3 – StudioPhotoDFlorez. 4–5 – Andrew Rybalko, Ground Picture, Lopolo, Sergey Novikov, Tartila, TinnaPong. 6–7 – AS Foodstudio, BAZA Production, Danicek, Jacek Chabraszewski, JeniFoto, LanaSweet, Lithiumphoto, norikko, Panimoni. 8–9 – Anastasiia Usenko. 10–11 – Anna Nahabed, JulsIst, MK photograp55, Nataly Studio, Red Fox studio, tairome, Volosina. 12–13 – Africa Studio, GOLDMAN99, hvostik, Katka Popova, Leeyakorn06, Miller Inna, Nora Hachio, Olena Chukhil, Olly Molly, Rvector, stockakia. 14–15 – Elena Schweitzer, Anastasi17, BestPhotoStudio, Canadapanda, Colorcocktail, Lana_Samcorp, M_Videous, Romanovskaya Darya, Sergey_Bogomyako, stockakia. 16–17 – Antonina Vlasova, Bernardo Emanuelle, Danielala, Igor Dutina, Karlisz, lukpedclub, planetzstudio, Sunnydream, ViDI Studio, Zhe Vasylieva. 18–19 – Andrii Bezvershenko, baldezh, BRO.vector, Jelena Aloskina, judyjump, KHON SUPAN, Nadezda Barkova, pilipphoto. 20–21 – Alexander Prokopenko, Antonina Vlasova, Craevschii Family, jamaludinyusuppp, Perfect_kebab, Steve Cukrov, Sunnydream. 22–23 – Ekateryna Zubal, FoxGrafy, KittyVector, Lalandrew, MarySan, Monkey Business Images, New Africa. 24–25 – Ground Picture, New Africa, Nina Firsova, Rob Byron, VectorShow. 26–27 – Aine, Bilanol, Clara Bastian, Dernkadel, hacohob, Natali Mart, paulaphoto, zealous. 28–29 – CGN089, Safety System. 30 – ben bryant, fizkes.

Library of Congress Cataloging-in-Publication Data is available at www.loc.gov or upon request from the publisher.

ISBN: 979-8-88916-459-3 (hardcover)
ISBN: 979-8-88916-464-7 (paperback)
ISBN: 979-8-88916-468-5 (ebook)

© 2024 BookLife Publishing
This edition is published by arrangement with BookLife Publishing.

North American adaptations © 2024 Bearport Publishing Company. All rights reserved. No part of this publication may be reproduced in whole or in part, stored in any retrieval system, or transmitted in any form or by any means, electronic, mechanical, photocopying, recording, or otherwise, without written permission from the publisher.

For more information, write to Bearport Publishing, 5357 Penn Avenue South, Minneapolis, MN 55419.

CONTENTS

Healthy Living 4
What Is a Diet? 6
A Balanced Plate 8
Vitamins and Minerals 10
Fruits and Vegetables 12
Carbohydrates 14
Proteins 16
Dairy and Alternatives 18
Fats 20
Water 22
Food Labels 24
Diverse Diets 26
A Healthy Planet 28
Making Choices 30
Glossary 31
Index 32
Read More 32
Learn More Online 32

Healthy Living

WHAT IS A LIFESTYLE?

Your lifestyle is the way that you live your life. The things you do each day, from what you eat to your favorite activities make up parts of your lifestyle.

A HEALTHY LIFESTYLE CAN HELP YOU FEEL HAPPIER AND STRONGER.

WHAT IS HEALTHY LIVING?

Healthy living means doing things to keep your mind and body feeling good. There are many ways to live well, but getting plenty of sleep and eating healthy food is a great place to start.

4

A HEALTHY MIND

Taking care of your mind is also important. Having healthy **relationships**, taking time to relax, and doing things you enjoy are great ways to keep your mind happy.

MAKING HEALTHY CHOICES

Your lifestyle is made up of the choices you make. What kinds of food do you eat? What do you do to make yourself happy? How do you stay active? You don't need to make the perfect choice every time to have a healthy lifestyle. However, it is important to understand how different choices might make you feel.

What is a Diet?

Your diet is the kinds of food that you usually eat and drink. It might be different from your friend's or your sister's. Fortunately, there are many ways to have a healthy diet.

DIFFERENT FOODS GIVE YOUR BODY DIFFERENT AMOUNTS AND TYPES OF **ENERGY**.

WHY DO I NEED FOOD?

Everything you do, from running around to sitting quietly, uses energy. All this energy needs fuel. The food you eat is turned into energy to fuel your body!

6

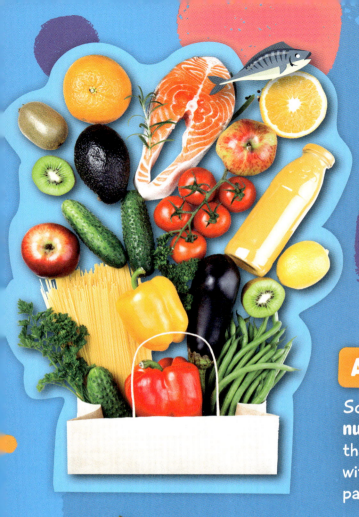

A HEALTHY DIET

Some food has more of the **nutrients** your body needs than others. Eating food with plenty of nutrients is part of a healthy diet.

IT'S ALL ABOUT BALANCE

A balanced diet is the best way to make sure your body gets what it needs to work. Usually, this means eating many different kinds of foods.

A BALANCED PLATE

Every day, your body needs different kinds of foods in different amounts to make up a balanced diet.

FOOD GROUPS

Foods are divided into different groups based on what they do for your body. The five main food groups are fruits, vegetables, grains, proteins, and dairy or dairy **alternatives**. Water is also important.

SOME MEALS YOU EAT MIGHT NOT HAVE FOOD FROM EACH GROUP. THAT'S OKAY. JUST BE SURE TO EAT FROM ALL THROUGHOUT THE DAY.

FRUITS

VEGETABLES

8

PROTEINS
This group includes meat, tofu, eggs, and seafood.

MAKING A BALANCED PLATE

This plate shows a balanced meal. You can use it as a tool to help you imagine what a balanced meal might look like. The plate doesn't show you how much food you should eat. Instead, it shows about what **percentage** of your plate each food group should take up.

DAIRY OR DAIRY ALTERNATIVES
This group has milk, yogurt, and cheese.

WATER

GRAINS
This group includes pasta, bread, and oatmeal.

Vitamins and Minerals

Vitamins and minerals are natural things that can be found in food. Your body needs them to grow and stay healthy. There are many kinds of vitamins and minerals. They all help your body in different ways.

What Are Vitamins?

Vitamins are made by plants and animals. The different vitamins help certain parts of your body work better. For example, vitamin A helps your eyes see colors and be able to better see in the dark. It can also help you fight off infections.

Carrots and green, leafy vegetables, such as kale and spinach, have lots of vitamin A.

WHAT ARE MINERALS?

Plants absorb minerals from soil and water. Animals get them by eating plants and other animals that have eaten plants. We get the mineral potassium from having dairy in our diets.

WHAT ARE VITAMIN PILLS?

Most of the time, people can get the vitamins and minerals they need from food. However, for some people this is not possible. They take pills that contain nutrients. Sometimes, these are called daily vitamins.

ONLY TAKE DAILY VITAMINS IF AN ADULT TELLS YOU TO.

Fruits and Vegetables

About half of your diet should be from the fruit and vegetable food groups. Luckily, there are many to choose from!

HAVE A TASTE TEST TO TRY NEW KINDS OF FRUITS AND VEGGIES!

MIX IT UP!

Different fruits and vegetables contain different vitamins and minerals. Be sure you eat a variety to give your body what it needs to keep feeling good.

WHAT COUNTS?

Which of your favorite foods are fruits and vegetables? Some things might surprise you!

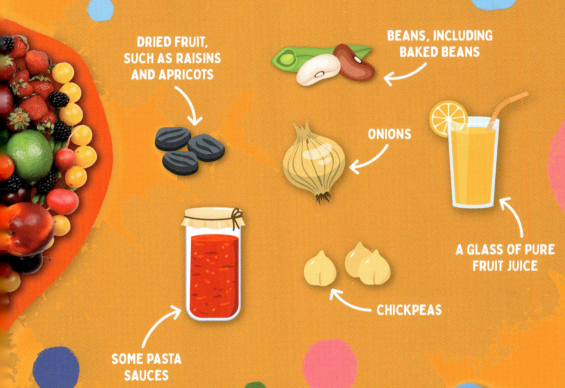

DRIED FRUIT, SUCH AS RAISINS AND APRICOTS

BEANS, INCLUDING BAKED BEANS

ONIONS

A GLASS OF PURE FRUIT JUICE

CHICKPEAS

SOME PASTA SAUCES

FITTING IN FRUITS AND VEGETABLES

There are many tasty ways to include plenty of fruits and veggies in your diet. Carrots and hummus make a great vegetable snack. You could freeze some fruit to make a cool and sweet summer treat.

Carbohydrates

Most of your body's energy comes from something in food called carbohydrates, or carbs. Carbs can be found in many foods including grains, beans, potatoes, and corn. There are different types of carbs, and some are better for you than others.

GRAINS

Types OF CARBOHYDRATES

There are two main types of carbs: complex carbohydrates and simple carbohydrates. Your body turns complex carbs into energy very slowly. This keeps you fuller longer and gives you energy that lasts a long time. Simple carbs provide fast energy. Your body breaks them down quickly but their energy doesn't last long.

COMPLEX CARBS

OATS

WHOLE GRAINS, SUCH AS QUINOA

FRUITS WITH LOTS OF FIBER, SUCH AS APPLES AND BANANAS

VEGETABLES WITH LOTS OF FIBER, SUCH AS BROCCOLI AND CARROTS

WHOLE GRAIN RICE

BEANS AND LENTILS

SIMPLE CARBS

BAKED GOODS, SUCH AS CAKES AND COOKIES

SUGARY BREAKFAST CEREALS

SUGARY DRINKS

SYRUP

GRAINS

Most of the carbs in your diet should come from the grains food group. Many grains are a source of complex carbohydrates that also contain fiber. Brown rice, oats, quinoa, and wheat are all great options.

FIBER IS A COMPLEX CARB THAT HELPS YOUR BODY **DIGEST** FOOD.

WHOLE GRAINS

Many foods made from grains come in a whole grain form as well as more processed options. Whole grain foods have more complex carbs, so choosing them will help keep you healthy and full of energy.

WHOLE GRAIN BREAD

WHITE BREAD

PROTEINS

Many parts of your body, including your **organs** and muscles, are made up of protein. Eating foods with lots of protein gives your body what it needs to grow and to repair itself when you get sick or injured.

PROTEIN PROVIDERS

Many foods contain protein. Some people get their protein by eating animals or animal products. Other people prefer to eat plants that have a lot of protein.

ANIMAL PROTEINS

ANIMAL PRODUCTS, SUCH AS EGGS

RED MEAT

WHITE MEAT

SEAFOOD

PLANT PROTEINS

GRAINS, SUCH AS QUINOA, OATS, AND BROWN RICE

LENTILS AND BEANS

SOY PRODUCTS, SUCH AS TOFU

NUTS AND NUT BUTTERS

PROTEIN AND OTHER FOOD GROUPS

Many protein-rich foods are also part of other food groups. Beans are a type of vegetable, but they also have lots of protein. Oats and brown rice have protein in them, but they are considered grains.

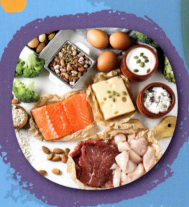

PLENTY OF PROTEIN

To have a balanced diet, eat different types of protein-rich foods. Most of the protein you eat should come from beans, nuts, fish, or white meat.

SOME PROTEIN-RICH FOODS HAVE MORE NUTRIENTS THAN OTHERS. IT'S IMPORTANT TO KEEP THIS IN MIND WHEN PICKING YOUR PROTEINS!

Dairy and Alternatives

Dairy foods, such as milk, cheese, and yogurt, are made using animal milk. Many of these foods are made with the milk from cows and goats. Dairy helps to keep your body strong.

Dairy-Free Diets

Some people choose not to eat dairy for health or ethical reasons. Fortunately, people can get many of the same benefits of dairy from alternative foods that have been **fortified**.

WHAT DOES DAIRY DO?

Dairy and dairy alternatives are good sources of vitamins and minerals, such as vitamin D and calcium. Calcium helps keep your teeth and bones strong. Many sources of dairy also contain lots of protein.

DO I GET ENOUGH?

There are a lot of ways to get dairy in your diet. Many different milk products are part of this food group. However, some milk products aren't because they have too little calcium and too much fat.

COUNTS AS PART OF THE DAIRY FOOD GROUP

MILK OR FORTIFIED ALTERNATIVE MILKS

YOGURT

MOST CHEESES

DOESN'T COUNT AS PART OF THE DAIRY FOOD GROUP

CREAM

CREAM CHEESE

BUTTER

FATS

Fat is an important part of your diet, too. It helps you feel full and can help your body absorb the nutrients it needs from other foods.

FATTY FOODS

Many foods have fat. You can often get the fats you need by eating the other foods you need. Most people don't have to worry about adding more fats on top of that.

UNSATURATED FATS

DIFFERENT TYPES OF FAT

There are different types of fat. The two types that are important for a healthy diet are called saturated and unsaturated fats. Unsaturated fats keep your heart healthy. Avocados, nuts, and salmon are all good sources of unsaturated fats. Saturated fats are less healthy. However, they are often found in foods that can help your body in other ways. Meat and milk contain lots of protein, but they also have saturated fats.

SATURATED FATS

Trans fat is made in a factory and put into many packaged foods. You don't need any of this kind of fat to stay healthy.

TRANS FATS ARE FOUND IN FOODS SUCH AS COOKIES. IT'S IMPORTANT NOT TO EAT TOO MUCH OF THIS FAT.

Water

Water keeps you **hydrated**, helps get rid of waste, keeps your organs working, and even helps control your body temperature.

MOST HUMANS CAN LIVE FOR ONLY A FEW DAYS WITHOUT WATER.

How Much Water?

The amount of water you need depends on what you do in a day. You'll need to drink more if you are exercising. When you are sick or somewhere hot, you will often need more water, too.

Different Drinks

If you are feeling thirsty, there are many different kinds of drinks to choose from. However, water helps you the most. Other drinks may contain sugar or **caffeine**, and they won't help you the same way water does.

Don't Forget to Drink!

There are many ways to make sure you drink plenty of water. Try carrying a reusable water bottle with you. That way, you can drink whenever you feel thirsty.

Try freezing some water in your bottle before you go to bed. Top it off with more water in the morning and you'll have icy water to go!

FOOD LABELS

Nutrition labels can be helpful when planning your meals and snacks. What will you find when you look at one of these labels?

SERVING INFORMATION
This tells you the size of one serving, as well as how many servings are in the package. The other information on the label is based on one serving.

PROTEIN
This part tells you how much protein is in the food.

VITAMINS AND MINERALS
The different types of vitamins and minerals are listed as well as their quantities.

Nutritio

8 servings per co
Serving size

Amount per serving
Calories

Total Fat 8g
Saturated Fat 1g
Trans Fat 0g
Cholesterol 0mg
Sodium 160mg
Total Carbohydra
Dietary Fiber 4g
Total Sugars 12g
Includes 10g A
Protein 3g

Vitamin D 2mcg
Calcium 260mg
Iron 8mg
Potassium 240mg

* The % Daily Value (DV) te
a serving of food contribut
a day is used for general r

THE PERCENTAGE (%) DAILY VALUE HELPS YOU KNOW IF YOU'RE GETTING ENOUGH OF THE RIGHT NUTRIENTS IN EACH SERVING. IT SHOWS A RECOMMENDED AMOUNT BASED ON AN AVERAGE DIET.

FAT

Food labels tell you how much fat is in the food. They also break down how much there is of different kinds of fats.

CARBOHYDRATES

Labels tell you the amount of carbs in a serving. Sometimes, they also show the different kinds of carbs in the food.

FOOD LABELS CAN BE CONFUSING. ASK AN ADULT FOR HELP IF YOU DON'T UNDERSTAND SOMETHING.

HOW DO FOOD LABELS HELP?

Food labels tell you which nutrients different foods have. They allow you to compare different foods so you can make healthy choices for a balanced diet.

Diverse Diets

With so many different foods to eat, it's no wonder we all have different diets. Some people might choose to avoid certain foods. Others are not able to eat some kinds of food because of **allergies** or intolerances.

ALLERGIES

An allergy is when the body has an unusually strong and harmful **reaction** to something. The most common allergens are milk, nuts, and shellfish. Some allergic reactions can be very serious and may require immediate medical attention.

People with very serious allergies may carry medicine with them in case they're accidentally exposed to the allergen.

INTOLERANCES

Food intolerances happen when the body struggles to digest certain things. Intolerances can make you feel sick or uncomfortable. The most common intolerances are to dairy and gluten.

There are many kinds of foods in each food group. Even if you have an allergy or intolerance, you can still have a balanced diet!

LIFESTYLE CHOICES

Some people may not eat certain foods because of personal choices. Vegetarians are people who choose not to eat meat or fish. Vegans choose not to eat meat, fish, or any other animal products, such as milk and eggs.

A HEALTHY PLANET

The foods you eat don't just affect your own health. They can also have a big impact on the health of the planet! In order for you to have all the foods you need for a healthy diet, Earth needs to be healthy, too.

HOW **FOOD** AFFECTS THE PLANET

Before it gets to your plate, all the food you eat has to be grown, raised, or made. This uses a lot of **resources**, including water, land, and fuel. It can also create lots of **greenhouse gases**, which aren't good for the planet.

PLANET-FRIENDLY FOODS

The more resources it takes to make a food, the larger the impact it will have on the planet. Foods that come from animals often use lots of resources. The animals need food, water, and places to live. Planet-friendly foods include fruits, vegetables, and grains. Many of these foods also have a lot of the important nutrients you need to stay healthy.

WASTE

Wasting food can be a problem, too. This happens if you forget to eat something before it goes bad. Planning out your meals before shopping can help you buy only what you need and avoid wasting food. If you have leftovers, you can save them in a container and eat them the next day.

Making Choices

A healthy lifestyle is all about making good choices. Try planning your meals to make sure you are taking care of your body. This will help you feel happy and healthy.

Are you excited to help plan a healthy diet?

Time for Treats

Some people think you have to eat a lot of boring foods to have a healthy diet. But that's not true! There are many yummy foods that are good for you. You can also eat foods that are tasty but not very nutritious as an occasional treat. It's all about balance!

GLOSSARY

allergies exaggerated reactions to things that do not have a strong effect on most people; allergens are things that cause an allergic reaction

alternatives other choices or options

caffeine a chemical often found in coffee, tea, and soda that acts as a stimulant

digest to break down food inside the body

energy the power used to move, grow, and live

fortified supplemented with vitamins and minerals to make food more nutritious

greenhouse gases gases in the air that trap heat around Earth

hydrated filled with enough water

nutrients vitamins, minerals, and other substances needed by living things for health and growth

organs parts of the body, such as the lungs or the heart, that do particular jobs

percentage a part of a whole, expressed as a number out of 100

reaction a response to something that happened

relationships the connections that people have with one another

resources things that are useful or valuable

INDEX

allergens 26
alternatives 8–9, 18–19
calcium 19
carbohydrates 14–15, 25
dairy 8–9, 11, 18–19, 27
energy 6, 14–15
fat 19–21, 25
fruit 8, 12–14, 29
grains 8–9, 14–17, 29
intolerances 26–27
labels 24–25
meat 9, 16–17, 21, 27
minerals 10–12, 19, 24
plate 8–9, 28
protein 8–9, 16–17, 19, 21, 24
vitamins 10–12, 19, 24

READ MORE

Martin, Claudia. *Food Warrior (Be a Waste Warrior!).* Minneapolis: Bearport Publishing Company, 2021.

Telesmanic, Shayna. *Food For You.* Beverly, MA: Quarto Library, 2022.

LEARN MORE ONLINE

1. Go to **www.factsurfer.com** or scan the QR code below.
2. Enter "**Healthy Diet**" into the search box.
3. Click on the cover of this book to see a list of websites.